Life on the Farm

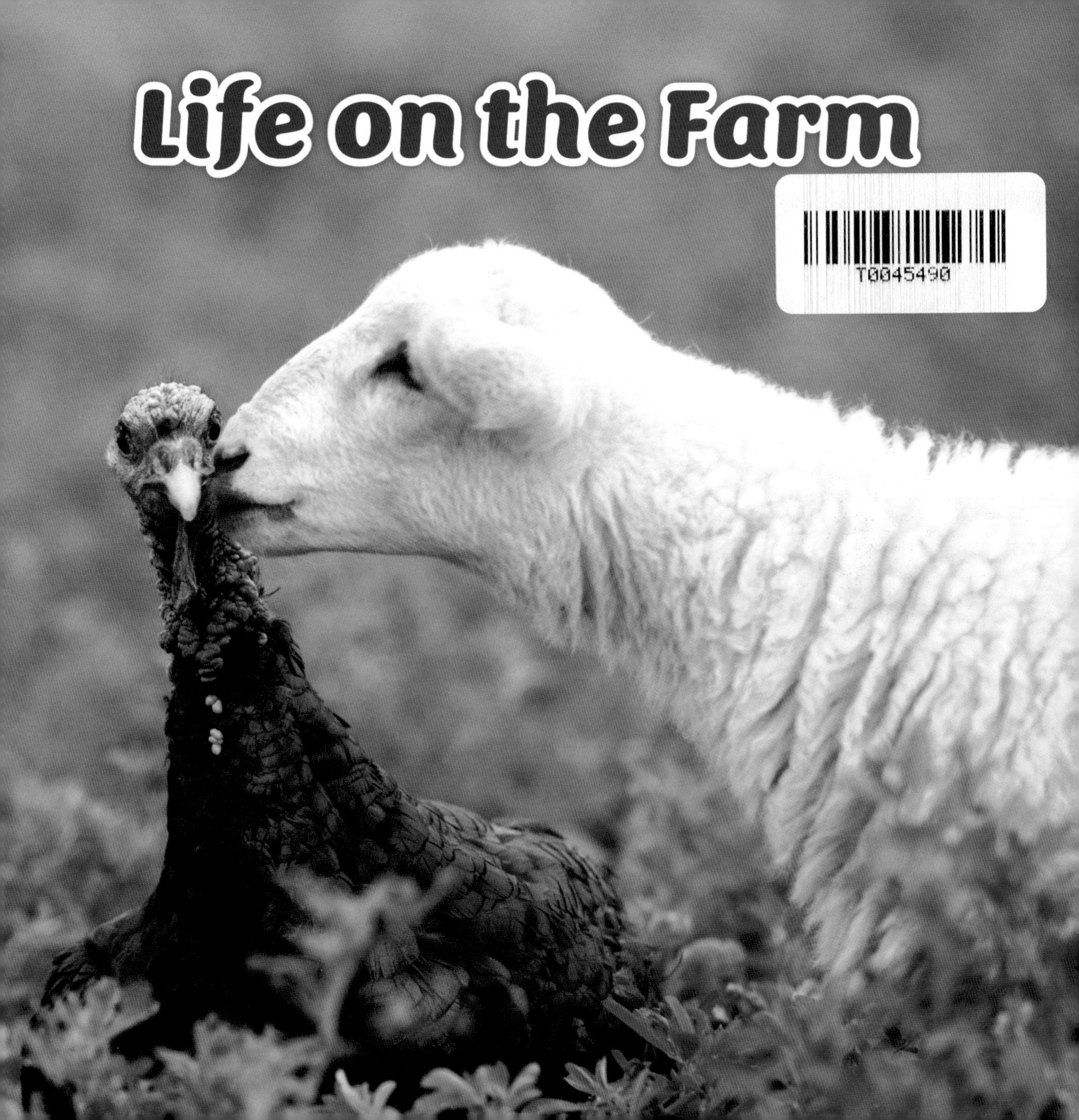

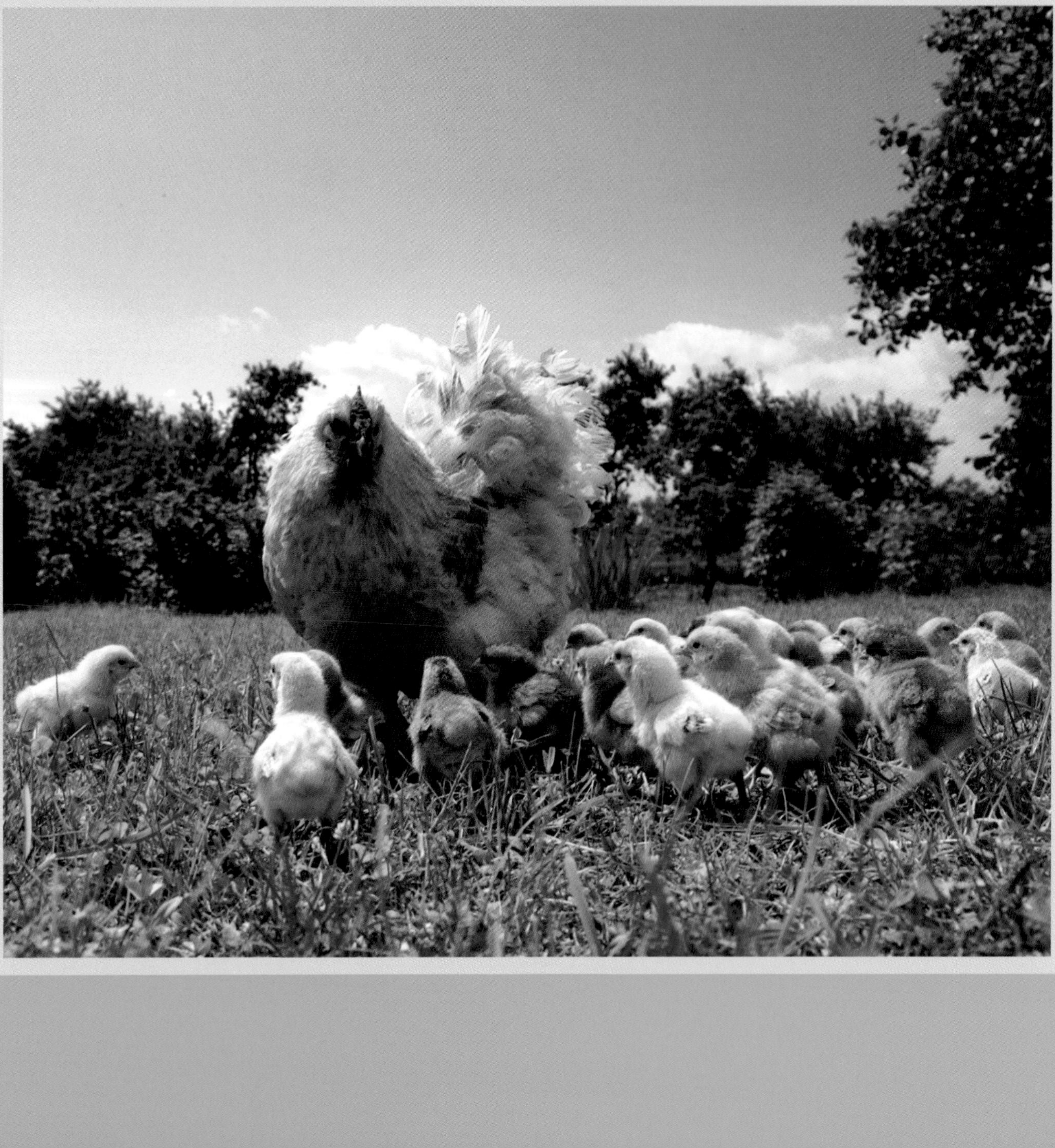

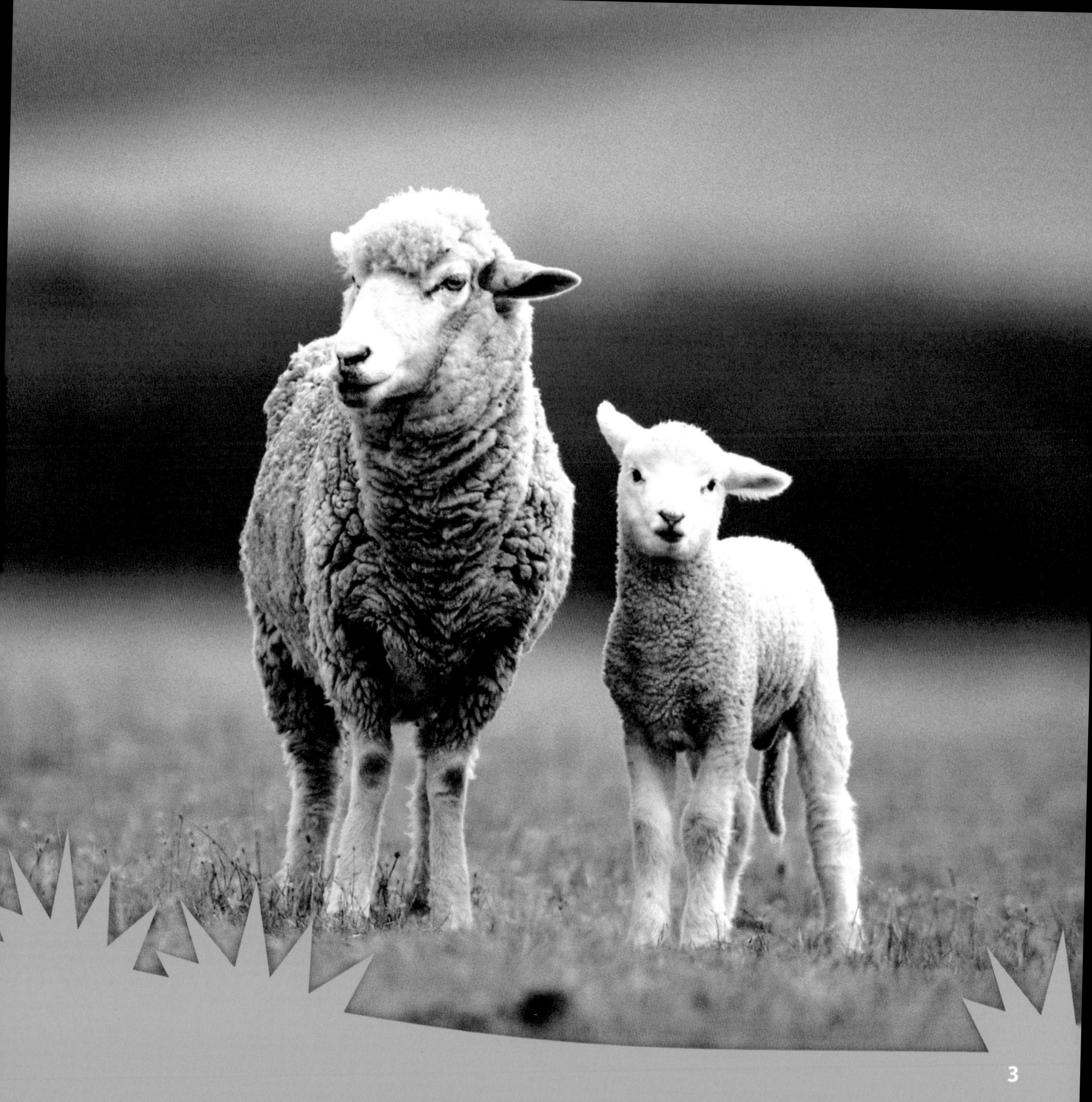

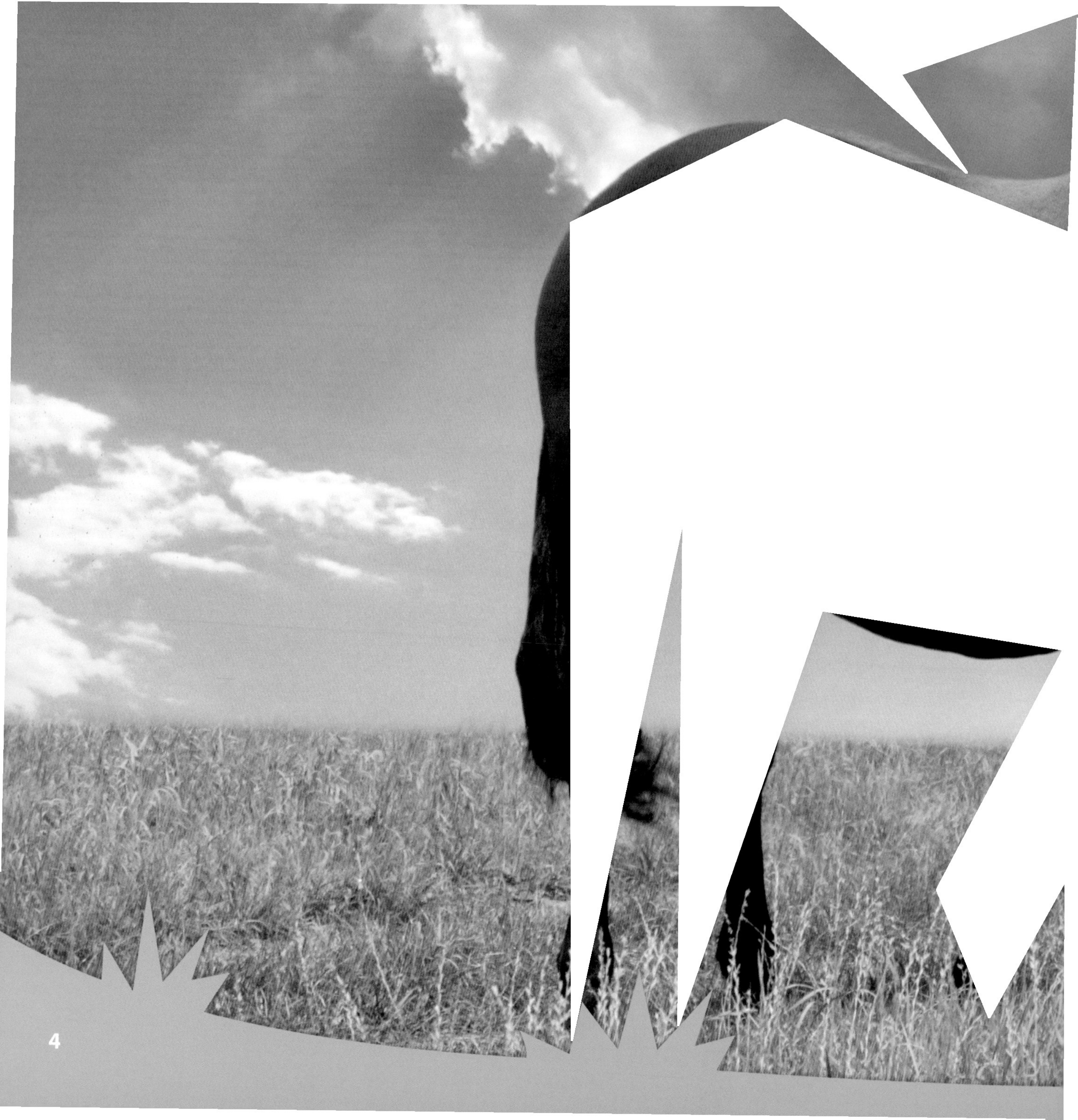

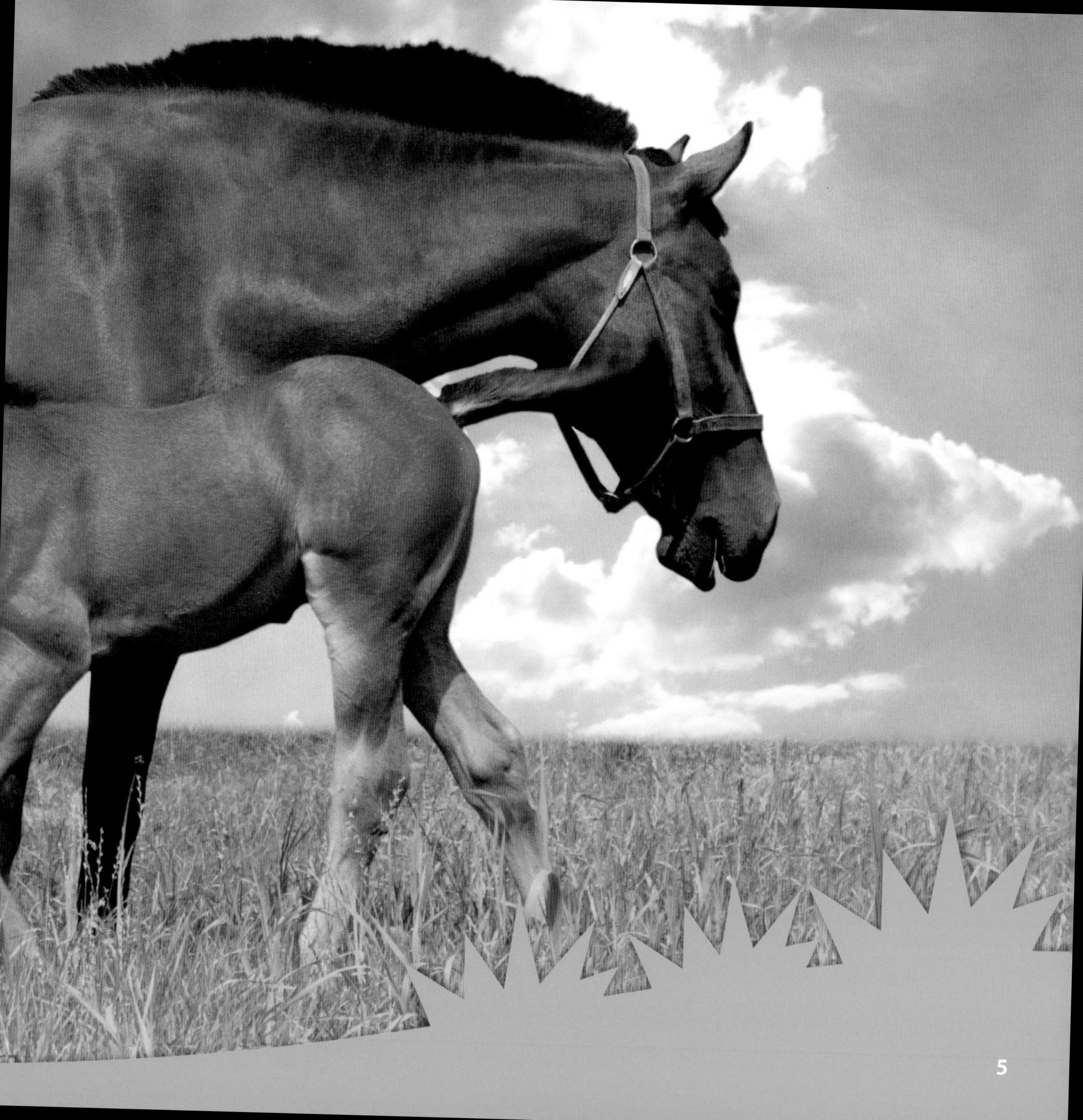

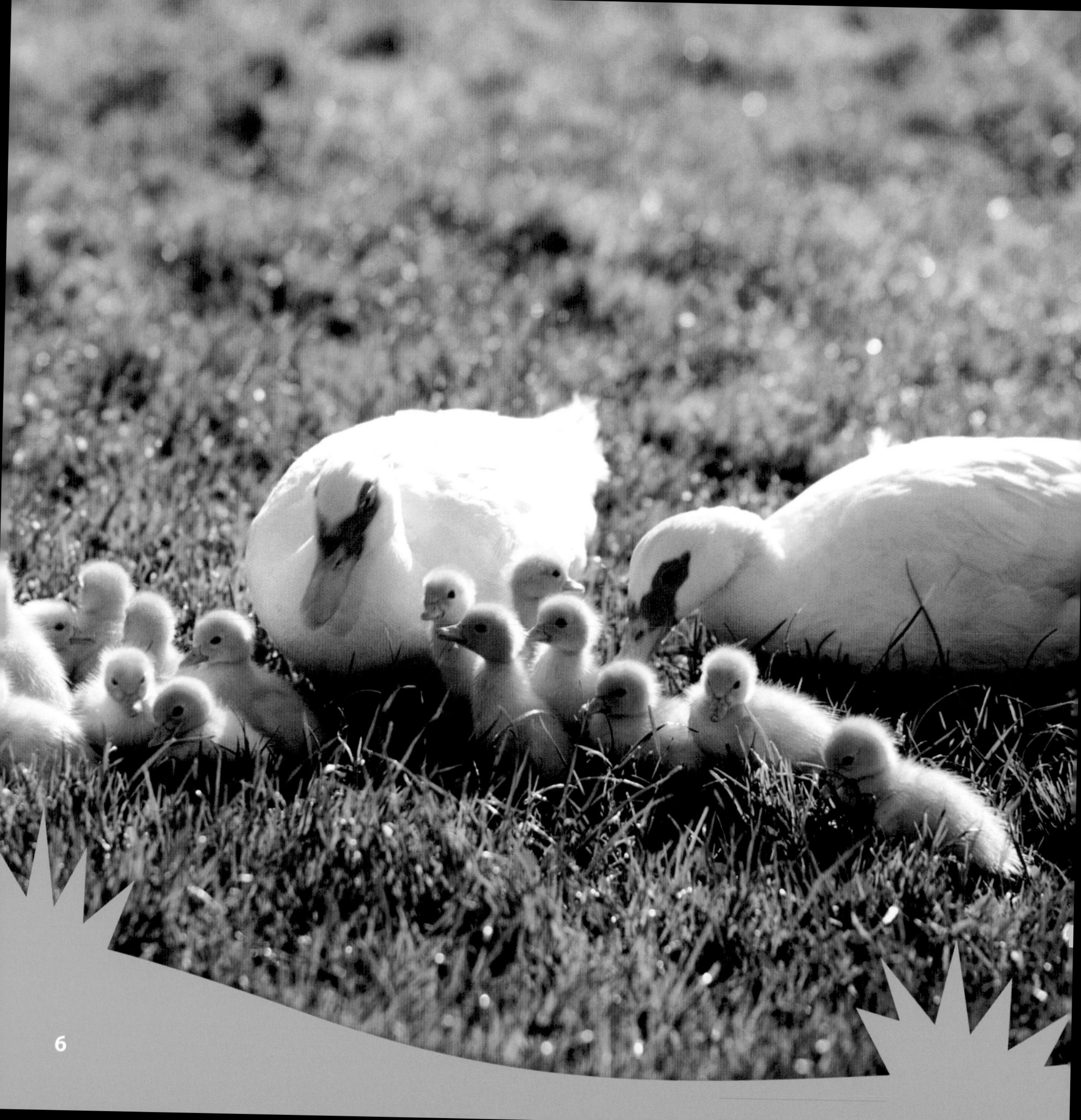

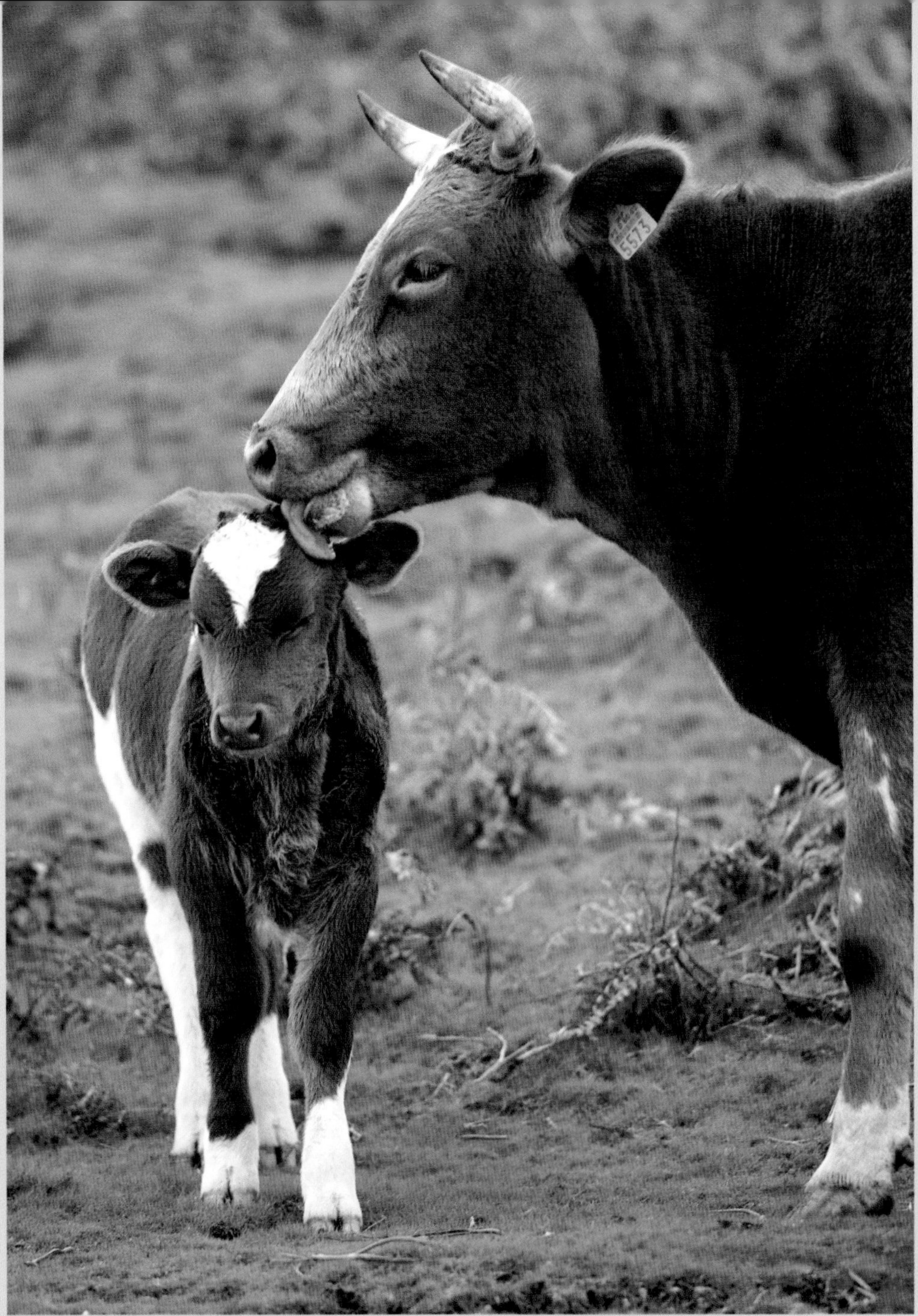

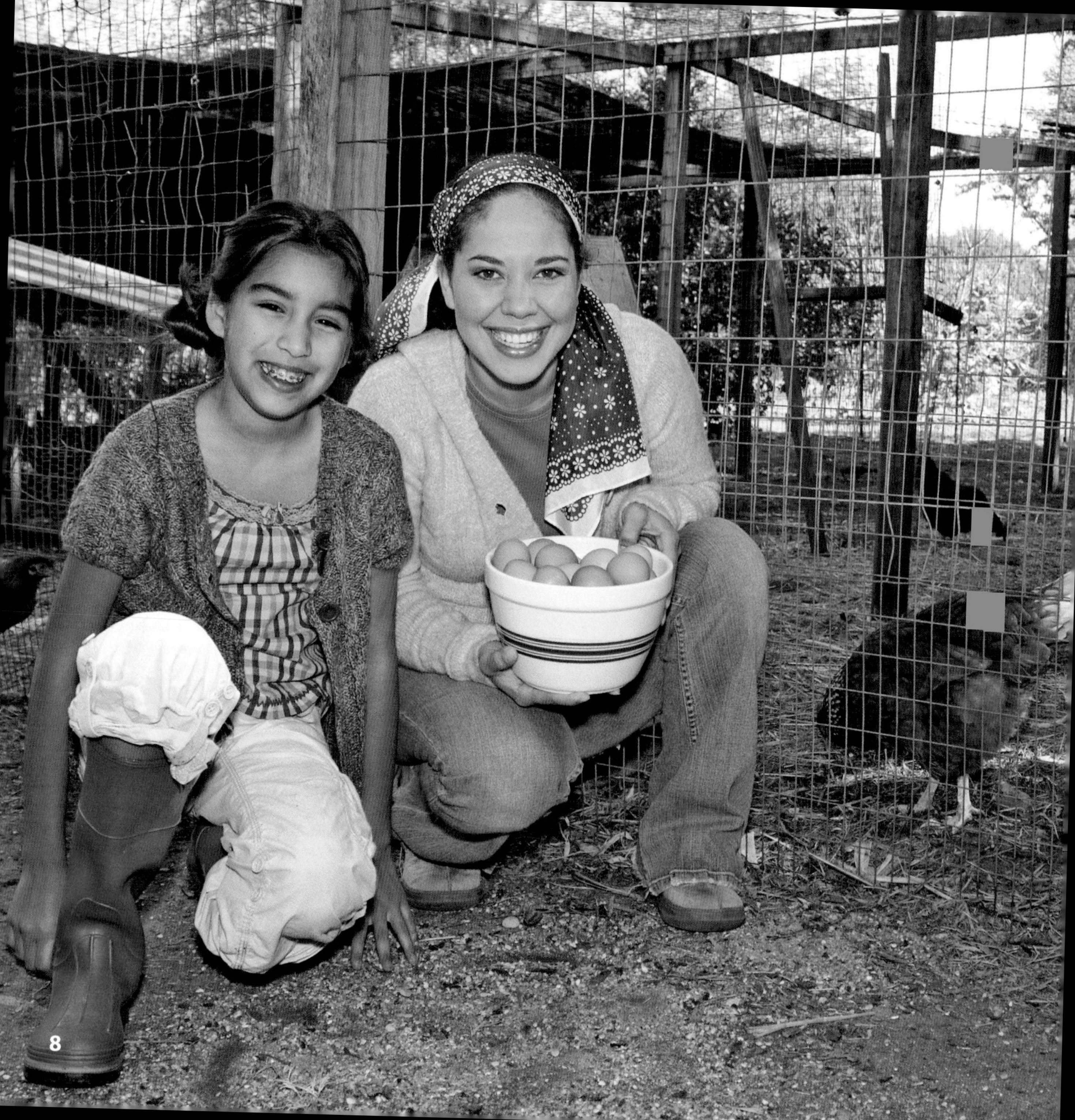